Greater Than a Tourist
Williamsburg
Virginia
United States of America

50 Travel Tips from a Local

Jeanne Croteau

Copyright © 2017 CZYK Publishing

All Rights Reserved. No part of this publication may be reproduced, including scanning and photocopying, or distributed in any form or by any means, electronic or mechanical, or stored in a database or retrieval system without prior written permission from the publisher.

Disclaimer: The publisher has put forth an effort in preparing and arranging this book. The information provided herein by the author is provided "as is". Use this information at your own risk. Consult your doctor before engaging in any medical activities. The publisher and author disclaim any liabilities for any loss of profit or commercial or personal damages resulting from the information contained in this book.

Order Information: To order this title please email lbrenenc@gmail.com or visit GreaterThanATourist.com. A bulk discount can be provided.

Cover Template Creator: Lisa Rusczyk Ed. D. using Canva.
Cover Creator: Lisa Rusczyk Ed. D.
Image: https://pixabay.com/en/governor-s-palace-williamsburg-1564033/

Lock Haven, PA
All rights reserved.
ISBN: 9781549792830

>TOURIST

Jeanne Croteau

BOOK DESCRIPTION

Are you excited about planning your next trip?

Do you want to try something new?

Would you like some guidance from a local?

If you answered yes to any of these questions, then this Greater Than a Tourist book is for you.

Greater Than a Tourist by Jeanne Croteau offers the inside scoop on Williamsburg, Virginia. Most travel books tell you how to sightsee. Although there's nothing wrong with that, as a part of the Greater than a Tourist series, this book will give you tips from someone who lives at your next travel destination. In these pages, you'll discover local advice that will help you throughout your trip.

Travel like a local. Slow down and get to know the people and the culture of a place. By the time you finish this book, you will be eager and prepared to travel to your next destination.

Jeanne Croteau

TABLE OF CONTENTS

BOOK DESCRIPTION

TABLE OF CONTENTS

DEDICATION

FROM THE PUBLISHER

WELCOME TO > TOURIST

INTRODUCTION

1. Walk Through History

2. Eat at The Cheese Shop

3. Visit the Governer's Palace

4. Tour the Campus of William & Mary

5. Pose on the Crim Dell Bridge

6. Cheer at a Tribe Football Game

7. Savor French Cuisine at The Blue Talon

8. Scream on a Ghost Tour

9. Dress Like a Colonialist

10. Shop at the Outlet Mall

11. Pass the Syrup at the Many Pancake Houses

Jeanne Croteau

12. Lick Your Finger's at Pierce's

13. Go Back in Time at the General Store

14. Get Scented at the World's Largest Yankee Candle Shop

15. Chill at Jamestown Beach

16. Seek Thrills at Busch Gardens

17. Sleep Like The Queen at Williamsburg Inn

18. Pose with Thomas Jefferson

19. Taste New Flavors at the International Food Festival

20. Slip and Slide at the Great Wolf Lodge

21. Feel Refined at the Local Wineries

22. Dig in to Tavern Fare

23. Swing on the LGPA Tournament Course at King's Mill

24. Get Festive at Christmas Town

25. Plunge Into Happiness at Water Country

26. Run on Duke of Gloucester Street

27. Play a Round of Mini Golf

28. Speak to George Washington

29. Buy a Tri-Corner Hat or Colonial Bonnet

30. Bruton Parish

31. Ride the Ferry Across the James River

32. Bike on the Capital Trail to Richmond

33. Leap with No Limits Skydiving

34. Sculpt at Williamsburg Pottery

35. Drive the Scenic Colonial Parkway

36. Get Cultured at the Muscarelle Museum

37. Shoot a Musket

38. Light Up Your Life at the Grand Illumination

39. Take a Picture in the Colonial Stocks

40. Move to the Sounds of the Fife and Drum Corps

41. Cool Down with a Treat From Sno to Go

42. Fill Up on Seafood at Captain George's

43. Speed Down a Zip Line at Go Ape!

44. Lap the Competition at Go-Karts Plus

45. Stock Up on Veggies at the Farmers Market

46. Search for Treasures at the Mermaid Bookstore

47. Be Inspired by the DeWitt Wallace Decorative Arts Museum

48. Sink Your Teeth into an Aberdeen Barn Steak

49. Enjoy the Local Craft Beers

50. Geek Out on History at Yorktown and Jamestown

Top Reasons to Book This Trip

Jeanne Croteau

WHERE WILL YOU TRAVEL TO NEXT?

Our Story

Notes

DEDICATION

This book is dedicated to College of William & Mary graduate, Joshua Leggette. Thank you for helping me love this city and for giving me three beautiful boys.

Jeanne Croteau

ABOUT THE AUTHOR

Jeanne Croteau is a psychology professor and writer who lives in Boise, Idaho. She loves to raising her six children to have an appreciation for nature, culture, and an active lifestyle.

From an early age, Jeanne has enjoyed traveling to new destinations across the globe but is particularly fond of Japan. This adventurous spirit has also motivated her to move to new areas including Virginia where she spent more than five years dividing her time between Richmond, Williamsburg, and Charlottesville.

Jeanne Croteau

HOW TO USE THIS BOOK

The Greater Than a Tourist book series was written by someone who has lived in an area for over three months. The goal of this book is to help travelers either dream or experience different locations by providing opinions from a local. The author has made suggestions based on their own experiences. Please do your own research before traveling to the area in case the suggested places are unavailable.

Jeanne Croteau

FROM THE PUBLISHER

Traveling can be one of the most important parts of a person's life. The anticipation and memories that you have are some of the best. As a publisher of the Greater Than a Tourist book series, as well as the popular 50 Things to Know book series, we strive to help you learn about new places, spark your imagination, and inspire you. Wherever you are and whatever you do I wish you safe, fun, and inspiring travel.

Lisa Rusczyk Ed. D.

CZYK Publishing

Jeanne Croteau

>TOURIST

WELCOME TO > TOURIST

Jeanne Croteau

INTRODUCTION

There are few other places in America that can claim to be as steeped in history as Williamsburg. Despite these connections to the country's earliest inhabitants, the area offers many modern delights, creating a uniquely diverse experience for locals and visitors alike. Allow this guidebook to give you an insider's perspective of Williamsburg and all of its wonders.

Jeanne Croteau

1. Walk Through History

Whether it's over modern sidewalks or well-preserved cobblestones, it's easy to walk through Williamsburg while taking in the historical sites including the Capitol, Courthouse, Bassett Hall and the Peyton Randolph House.

The area experiences all four seasons, including hot, humid, and rainy summers and occasionally snowy winters. It's best to cover your bases and plan for anything in Virginia!

2. Eat at The Cheese Shop

The Cheese Shop is located in Merchant's Square, right in the middle of downtown Williamsburg. Finding a parking spot can be difficult so be prepared to walk a few blocks. Fortunately, the food at The Cheese Shop is entirely worth it.

In addition to a very busy deli counter offering sandwiches at the back, the store offers a variety of cured meats, cheeses, and other snacks. Seating is very limited but there are outdoor tables and benches located nearby.

3. Visit the Governor's Palace

As you make your way down Duke of Gloucester street, you won't be able to miss the Governor's Palace. The expansive grounds and surrounding greenery help give it a majestic presence.

Until the state capital moved to Richmond, the estate served as the residence of the Royal Governors of the Colony of Virginia, and was once the home of both Patrick Henry and Thomas Jefferson.

4. Tour the Campus of William & Mary

The College of William & Mary is the second-oldest school of higher education in the country and allows visitors to not only tour the grounds but also notable classrooms, halls, and the Wren Chapel.

Founded in 1693, graduates of William & Mary include George Washington, Jon Stewart, and Pittsburgh Steelers coach, Mike Tomlin.

5. Pose on the Crim Dell Bridge

Tucked into a wooded area, the Crim Dell bridge is a picturesque spot that has served as a backdrop for many couples who are getting engaged.

In fact, it's fabled that if you kiss someone while crossing the bridge, you are destined to be married and the only way to break the spell is to throw them over the side!

6. Cheer at a Tribe Football Game

If you enjoy tailgating, you'll love the scene around Zable Stadium before each William & Mary Tribe football game.

It may not be the largest facility in the country but it recently received a facelift in the form of state-of-the-art press boxes, concession stands, and suites for the ultimate fan experience. Don't forget to give Griffin, the team mascot, a high-five!

7. Savor French Cuisine at Blue Talon Bistro

For the ultimate in comfort food with a French flair, there is no better place than Blue Talon Bistro. Open for breakfast, lunch, and dinner, guests can sample from small plates, charcuterie platters, and mouthwatering entrees, among other items, on the extensive menu.

Reservations are strongly recommended and parking is limited so be sure to plan accordingly!

8. Scream on a Ghost Tour

Williamsburg is part of the oldest area in America. As a result, there are many spooky tales that are associated with those earliest days when the settlers first arrived and fought on the shores.

There are many great ghost tour companies but the oldest, The Original Ghosts of Williamsburg Tour, has been sending chills down people's spines for more than 26 years.

9. Dress For the Occasion

It's one thing to visit Colonial Williamsburg and learn about the history but it's quite another to completely immerse yourself in the period.

Incredibly, the Visitor's Center offers costume rentals so that visitors can get the full experience. There are a variety of items and styles to choose from, which only adds to the fun!

10. Shop at the Outlet Mall

If you need a break from the historic surroundings, you can look for something modern and new at the Williamsburg Premium Outlets.

The shops range from clothing and shoes to electronics and kitchenware – and everything in between.

A food court, snack shops throughout the mall, and nearby restaurants will help keep hunger at bay while you shop till you drop!

>TOURIST

Duke of Gloucester Street "rightly can be called the most historic avenue in all America."

Franklin D. Roosevelt

Jeanne Croteau

11. Pass the Syrup at the Many Pancake Houses

There is no shortage of pancake houses in Williamsburg. If you are a fan of the fluffy, sweet, breakfast food, you will find yourself with many options from which to choose.

In fact, according to the National Pancake House website, Williamsburg "has more pancake houses and pancake restaurants per capita than any other place in the United States."

With so much competition, they all try to be the best so it's quite possible that you will never have a better pancake breakfast than you can have in Williamsburg.

12. Lick Your Fingers at Pierce's

Virginia is the beginning of the south and, if there's one thing the region is known for, it's delicious southern comfort food. If you are craving some good eats, look no further than Pierce's Pitt Bar-B-Que.

Conveniently located right off the 64 highway, it's a meat lover's dream with a menu offering smoked ribs, chicken, burgers, hot dogs, and sandwiches. The sides are equally impressive and regional including collard greens, Brunswick stew, and hushpuppies.

If you're coming as a family, there are several great kids meals from which to choose. Don't forget dessert! Pierce's offers delicious baked good that everyone can enjoy!

13. Go Back in Time at the General Store

You will feel just like you stepped back in time when you pull up to the Williamsburg General Store. Located right on Richmond Rd. near the Premium Outlets Mall and restaurants, the store is easy to include in your plans for the day.

Inside, you will find a wide variety of items ranging from quaint, rustic household goods to gag gifts and patriotic fare.

As an added bonus, the General Store features an ice cream parlor all the way at the back where you will find cones, milk shakes, and other goodies. Seating is very limited to be prepared to take your treats to go.

14. Get Scented at the World's Largest Yankee Candle Shop

Most of us have walked past a Yankee Candle Shop. Usually, they are small storefronts located in malls that smell great and sell candles. Pretty simple.

The location in Williamsburg, however, is a game-changer. It's the largest Yankee Candle Shop in the country and offers so much more than scented wax in a jar.

Year round, there are numerous events to please patrons including a Girls Night Out, Village Festival, and Christmas activities.

15. Chill at Jamestown Beach

There's a time for walking the streets and taking in the sights and then there's a time to kick back and chill. Fortunately, visitors to Williamsburg won't have to travel far to get to Jamestown Beach.

In just a short 10-minute drive, you'll be looking out over the James River and sinking your toes into the sand on this freshwater beach. You can pack a lunch or enjoy many of the nearby amenities. It really is an oasis in the middle of the concrete jungle.

16. Seek Thrills at Busch Gardens

Thrill seekers of all ages will find something to do at Busch Gardens. Sprawling across 383 acres and featuring areas devoted to different countries around the world, The National Amusement Park Historical Association has named it "the world's most beautiful theme park" every year since 1990.

The Sesame Street Forest of Fun and children's areas will delight young patrons while more adventurous rides, such as The Griffon, will leave older riders breathless.

In addition to the usual amusement park offerings, Busch Gardens has yearly, seasonal events including Howl-O-Scream and Christmas Town.

17. Sleep Like the Queen at Williamsburg Inn

To experience one of the finest, largest, historic resort hotels in the country, book a room at the Williamsburg Inn – even if it's just for one night!

Added to the National Register of Historic Places in 1997, the landmark property has boasted, at least, one very famous guest – the Queen of England!

Known for its outstanding service and cuisine, the Williamsburg Inn hosted Her Majesty Queen Elizabeth II and His Royal Highness Prince Philip, Duke of Edinburgh, in both 1957 and 2007.

18. Pose with Thomas Jefferson

If you're strolling around Merchant's Square after dining at Blue Talon Bistro, The Cheese Shop, or shopping at the many local stores, you might notice someone is already occupying one of the street benches and looks like he's been there for quite some time!

A statue of Thomas Jefferson attracts many people who opt to take a picture sitting next to the third president of the United States of America and the author of the Declaration of Independence.

19. Taste New Flavors at the International Food Festival

Are you looking for an adventure for your taste buds? The Food & Wine Festival usually takes place over the summer and is included in the price of admission to Busch Gardens.

Foodies will love being able to sample fare from different parts of the world. The affordable menu includes items that are not normally available at the park and offers a rare opportunity to enjoy authentic, exotic tastes from multiple vendors.

20. Slip and Slide at the Great Wolf Lodge

People, especially families with young children, go absolutely crazy for Great Wolf Lodge. The hotel is built around a massive indoor water park and many spend entire days in or around the pool.

While it can get pricey to stay at this chain resort, the Williamsburg location regularly has deals and promotions offered through their official website. Whether it's reduced nightly rates or dining credit, there are ways to save money while living big!

>TOURIST

"Many a night, late, I'd walk down Duke of Gloucester Street from the Wren Building to the Capitol. On those walks, in the dark, I felt the spirit of the patriots who created a free and independent country, who helped birth it right here in Williamsburg. It was on those walks that I made my commitment to public service."

Robert M. Gates, Former Secretary of Defense

Jeanne Croteau

21. Feel Refined at the Local Wineries

Along the Colonial Wine Trail, would-be sommeliers can visit any of the four local wineries along the Interstate 64 corridor including Saude Creek Vineyards in Lanexa, New Kent Winery in New Kent and James River Cellars in Richmond, just an hour away.

Those who prefer to stay put can sit, sip, and take in the scenery at Williamsburg Winery, which is surrounded by more than 50 acres of scenic vineyards.

22. Dig into Tavern Fare

Take your taste buds on a tour of history by ducking in to one of the area's taverns. In the Colonial Williamsburg area, visitors can choose from Chowning's, King's Arms, Shields, or Christiana Campbell's Tavern, which was George Washington's favorite place for seafood!

Whether it's a family meal, date night, or a special occasion, there's a little something for everyone.

23. Swing on the LPGA Tournament Course at Kingsmill

Fancy a round of golf? If so, you're in luck! Williamsburg's Kingsmill Resort is an impressive golf destination where guests can choose from The Plantation Course or The River Course which hosts the world's best PGA and LPGA players. In addition to golf, Kingsmill offers top-notch accommodations, recreation, a spa, several restaurants, and even wedding packages.

24. Get Festive at Christmas Town

While Virginia weather never stays very cold, Busch Gardens does close its rides during the winter. An exception, of course, is when it opens for several weeks during the holiday season.

If, during the regular season, Busch Gardens is considered "the most beautiful theme park in the world," you can only imagine how spectacular it becomes for Christmas Town.

Aglow with more than eight million lights, it is officially the largest Christmas display in North America. Guests can warm up with festive food and drink (including the park's signature peppermint fudge hot chocolate) while enjoying a handful of kid-friendly areas as well as a few thrill rides.

25. Plunge into Happiness at Water Country

It can get pretty hot and humid in Williamsburg so there's no better way to cool off than at Virginia's largest water park!

Water Country USA boasts impressive water slides and raft rides, as well as pools and lazy rivers. Tackle the wave pool and then retreat to a lounge chair or private cabana that you can rent from the park.

It's not just fun and games, though. You can also take swimming lessons and take classes to become a certified lifeguard too!

26. Run on Duke of Gloucester Street

When Williamsburg was founded back in 1632, it was decided that the main street running through the city would be named in the honor of his Highness William Duke of Gloucester. When it was restored more than 200 years later, then-President Franklin D. Roosevelt said that it could "rightly can be called the most historic avenue in all America."

Since then, it has become a popular place for locals and visitors to walk and take their morning runs. Famous people who have strolled down Duke of Gloucester include Former president, Bill Clinton, and former Secretary of State, Hillary Clinton, as well as Ronald Reagan and Winston Churchill.

27. Play a Round of Mini Golf

Despite being a relatively small city, Williamsburg has several great places where you can play a round of miniature golf.

Among the most popular is Pirate's Cove Adventure Golf which features a pirate theme complete with waterfalls and caves. Another option is Go-Karts Plus which, in addition to mini golf, also offers bumper cars and boats, go-karts, and attractions for visitors of all ages.

28. Speak to George Washington

One of the most fun things about Colonial Williamsburg are the reenactors that you will encounter on the street. Whether it's a soldier or a historical figure, the actors stay in character and do their best to represent the time period.

While it's not quite the same as the real thing, you might find yourself carrying on a conversation with George Washington or, at least, someone portraying the first American president. If you find yourself in a similar situation, play along and suspend reality for a few minutes. You'll never forget this unique experience!

29. Buy a Tricorn Hat or Colonial Bonnet

In the shops along the streets in Colonial Williamsburg and, certainly, in the Visitor's Center, you will find any number of souvenirs. While some may opt for a keychain or a magnet, you might want to take home something more elaborate.

You will discover that vendors sell tricorn hats and bonnets that were characteristic of those earliest days in Williamsburg and you will be hard-pressed to find them outside of the area.

They could look great in a display case or on your mantle but, with a few additional clothing items, you could end up putting on your very own reenactments at home!

30. Worship at Bruton Parish Church

Williamsburg's Bruton Parish Church has a very long history. First built in 1660, it served as a place of worship for Thomas Jefferson, Patrick Henry, George Washington, and many others.

There are notable people, including Governor Francis Fauquier, who are actually buried beneath the structure which also served as a hospital during the Battle of Yorktown and the Civil War.

It has been restored a couple times in the 20th century and continues to offer worship services throughout the week.

"I have so many cherished memories of William and Mary over the years – of the faculty and especially the students – and will always look back on my time as Chancellor with great happiness."

Margaret Thatcher, Former British Prime Minister

Jeanne Croteau

31. Ride the Ferry Across the James River

In a world full of upcharges and blackout dates, you might be shocked by the fact that the Jamestown-Scotland Ferry runs 24 hours a day, 365 days of the year (including holidays!) and is absolutely free! How amazing is that?

The four ferry boats, (the Virginia, Williamsburg, Surry, and Pocahontas) were built between 1936 and 1995 and can carry from 28 to 70 cars at a time.

While the short boat ride between Surry and Williamsburg is typically pretty smooth, the waters can be choppy sometimes. Also, since it is free, the lines can be long during peak hours which run from 6:00-8:00am and 4:00-6:00pm every day.

32. Bike on the Capital Trail to Richmond

The first capital of Virginia was Williamsburg. The current capital of Virginia is Richmond. Wouldn't it be great if you could bike on a path that connects them? The good news is, you can!

This incredibly scenic route features approximately 52 miles of paved trails that run along the Route 5 corridor. It's hard to imagine a more beautiful and historic way to travel between these two important cities. As a bonus, you'll get a great workout!

33. Leap with No Limits Skydiving

Have you ever wanted to jump out of a plane? If skydiving is on your bucket list, there are several services in the Williamsburg area that you could try but No Limits Skydiving has the best prices and specializes in first-time and tandem jumpers.

See the historic triangle of Williamsburg, Jamestown, and Yorktown from high in the sky as you freefall at 120mph! You can even get a copy of the video capturing your experience from your plane ride all the way down until you are safely on the ground!

34. Williamsburg Pottery

Nearly 80 years ago, the first Williamsburg Pottery opened and focused solely on high-quality, reproduction salt glaze pieces. Today, it has grown into so much more.

In 2012, the business moved to a new location where it could spread its wings and offer three types of marketplaces for Gourmet Kitchen, Home Essentials, and Outdoor Living. To further elevate the experience for guests, the space also includes a standalone Au Bon Pain restaurant.

Closed only on Christmas Day, Williamsburg Pottery focuses on offering locally grown, mostly made in America items in addition to a collection of international goods.

35. Drive the Scenic Colonial Parkway

Want to see all three points of Virginia's historic triangle while avoiding the crowds and taking in the scenery? Hit the Colonial Parkway that connects Williamsburg to Jamestown and Yorktown.

Stretching across a picturesque 23 miles, you'll go from the York River to the James River while seeing all of the natural beauty in between.

Completed in 1957, the National Park Service managed to construct the three-lane Parkway while preserving the environment and protecting wildlife.

36. Get Cultured at the Muscarelle Museum

Located within Lamberson Hall on the campus of The College of William and Mary, the Muscarelle Museum of Art is a working laboratory that serves as a platform for the institution's carefully curated collections as well as visiting exhibits.

Initially, the Museum's aim was to foster an artistic spirit within The College's students but it quickly evolved into model for the entire surrounding community.

Established in 1732, the already impressive Muscarelle Museum of Art will offer even more to patrons as it prepares to move to a new arts complex which will be designed by internationally renowned architectural firm, Pelli Clarke Pelli.

37. Shoot a Musket

Colonial Williamsburg Musket Range gives visitors the opportunity to handle two different reproduction 18th-century firearms from the Revolutionary War period at the Williamsburg Lodge.

Since you will be firing live rounds at a target, you will be required to present a photo ID and sign a waiver. Guests aged 14-17 can participate as long as they are being supervised by a legally responsible adult who is not shooting at the range.

The experience, which requires its own admission ticket, includes transportation to and from the range, detailed instructions, safety equipment, targets, and ammunition.

38. Light Up Your Life at the Grand Illumination

To mark the beginning of the holiday season, Colonial Williamsburg puts on quite a show. In addition to the many colorful and unique decorations that can be seen throughout the Revolutionary City, locals and visitors alike are also treated to musical performances and a spectacular fireworks display from the Capital, Magazine, and the Governor's Palace.

The Grand Illumination reflects those that took place in the 18th century when Virginians would fire guns or set off fireworks to commemorate a special occasion such as a military victory or the welcoming of a new colonial governor.

39. Take a Picture in the Colonial Stocks

In colonial times, sturdy wooden stocks were used as a form of punishment and public humiliation, particularly for those who were accused of engaging in sinful behavior (such as a man kissing his wife in public!).

Today, the stocks, along with other disciplinary devices such as a pillory and whipping post, still stand in Colonial Williamsburg giving guests an opportunity to take an up-close look as well as snap a photo or two.

40. Wax Patriotic With the Fife and Drum Corps

Incredibly, as Virginia prepared for the British Invasion back in 1775, Fifers and Drummers, who were typically boys between ages 10-18, were enlisted alongside soldiers and were considered an integral part of the military.

Today, the Fife and Drum Corps is comprised of both boys and girls in that age group who are selected from a lengthy waiting list at age 10 and continue to train and practice military music weekly for the next eight years until they graduate from high school. These magnificent and dedicated field musicians put on more than 700 performances in Colonial Williamsburg each year.

>TOURIST

"Colonial Williamsburg is an important piece of America that everyone should experience."

Tom Hanks

Jeanne Croteau

41. Cool Down with a Treat From Sno to Go

It can get pretty hot and muggy in Williamsburg and, while you should carry a water bottle, another great way to beat the heat is at Sno to Go.

Famous for their shaved-ice snoballs, Sno to Go offers a wide variety of syrup flavors that can be mixed and customized. They also sell soft serve ice cream, sundaes, shakes, floats, and other cold drinks.

42. Fill Up on Seafood at Captain George's

Whether you're dining alone or as a family, one of the greatest seafood restaurants in the Williamsburg area is Captain George's.

Located within a charming brick building and featuring a fun nautical theme, the restaurant is listed in the Top 12 All-You-Can-Eat Seafood Buffets in America!

With a seating capacity of up to 900 people, Captain George's can accommodate large groups and has spent more than 35 years perfecting its recipes for everything from Alaskan snow crab legs to slow-roasted prime rib.

43. Speed Down a Zipline at Go Ape!

Go Ape! has several locations across the country but the one in Williamsburg features two outdoor adventures and is a two to three hour excursion suitable for the whole family.

The Go Ape Treetop Adventure will take guests through five obstacle courses and 37 exhilarating crossings including a trapeze, Tarzan swings, and multiple zip lines!

While these action-packed courses may be a lot of fun, they might not be suitable for young guests. Fortunately, Go Ape! has Treetop Junior course for children 10 years of age and under so that they can get in on the action with age-appropriate challenges.

44. Lap the Competition at Go-Karts Plus

As the name suggests, Go-Karts Plus does feature go-karts but there's also so much more to do. In addition to mini golf, the venue boasts bumper cars and boats, the Disk'o thrill ride, a shooting gallery, and a kiddie coaster.

If you are looking for something a little slower-paced after all the excitement, you can pan for gemstones and fossils or hit the arcade. There's even a playground area for toddlers looking to run, climb, and slide!

45. Stock Up on Veggies at the Farmer's Market

Since 2002, the Williamsburg Farmer's Market has united 40 vendors who bring fresh produce to the area on any given Saturday throughout the entire year.

Featuring live music, baked goods, and other prepared foods, local, fresh goods bring the community together at the market which is conveniently located in Merchant's Square.

46. Search for Treasures at the Mermaid Bookstore

Bibliophiles will love the Mermaid Bookstore which offers an eclectic selection of new, used, and rare books in a whimsical and enchanting location. Continually evolving, guests will find that this fun shop is never the same from one visit to the next.

Founded in 1977 and located in a basement beneath an ice cream shop, the quirky bookstore is conveniently located adjacent to the Historic Area of Colonial Williamsburg and beautiful Merchants Square.

47. Be Inspired by the DeWitt Wallace Decorative Arts Museum

Opened in 1985, the DeWitt Wallace Decorative Arts Museum is younger than many of the historic buildings and sites in the Williamsburg area but this venue is jam packed with the finer things from the 17th, 18th, and 19th centuries.

With 15 galleries, the museum showcases the world's largest collection of southern furniture, metals, glass, paintings, prints, textiles, and firearms from yesteryear. Additionally, it is home to one of the most extensive collections of British ceramics outside of England.

48. Sink Your Teeth Into Fat Canary

If you are looking for the very finest in fine dining that Williamsburg has to offer, you must pay a visit to Fat Canary. Not only do locals rave about the food but the restaurant has earned the AAA Four Diamond award every single year since opening in 2003. It's just that good.

The seasonal menu changes regularly in order to bring guests the very freshest, in-season meals possible. Plus, you will feel right at home at the Fat Canary which is owned and managed by the Power family who also own The Cheese Shop.

49. Enjoy Local Craft Beers

It might not be a major city but Williamsburg has become a great place to sample a craft beer. In fact, the area is home to nationally-recognized AleWerks Brewing Company, one of Virginia's leading microbreweries.

In the spring, check out the Williamsburg Craft Beer Festival, an event that also includes great food and live music, while supporting local non-profit organizations.

50. Geek Out on History at Yorktown and Jamestown

Williamsburg is part of the historic triangle along with Jamestown and Yorktown. To fully round out your experience, consider making the rounds by seeing these nearby attractions.

Visitors can explore the Jamestown Settlement or the American Revolution Museum at Yorktown, which each have their own admission prices, but it might be worth purchasing one of the many combination tickets that grant access to all of the sites.

Top Reasons to Book This Trip

- History: See where America began.

- Food: From barbecue to ice cream, the food is amazing.

- Beach: Clean, freshwater on sandy shores.

- Shopping: Souvenirs and an outlet mall that has it all.

Jeanne Croteau

>TOURIST

GREATER THAN A TOURIST

Visit GreaterThanATourist.com
http://GreaterThanATourist.com

Sign up for the Greater Than a Tourist Newsletter
http://eepurl.com/cxspyf

Follow us on Facebook:
https://www.facebook.com/GreaterThanATourist

Follow us on Pinterest:
http://pinterest.com/GreaterThanATourist

Follow us on Instagram:
http://Instagram.com/GreaterThanATourist

Jeanne Croteau

> TOURIST

GREATER THAN A TOURIST

Please leave your honest review of this book on Amazon and Goodreads. Thank you.

We appreciate your positive and negative feedback as we try to provide tourist guidance in their next trip from a local.

> TOURIST

GREATER THAN A TOURIST

Our Story

Traveling is a passion of the "Greater than a Tourist" series creator. Lisa studied abroad in college, and for their honeymoon Lisa and her husband toured Europe. During her travels to Malta, an older man tried to give her some advice based on his own experience living on the island since he was a young boy. She was not sure if she should talk to the stranger but was interested in his advice. When traveling to some places she was wary to talk to locals because she was afraid that they weren't being genuine. Through her travels, Lisa learned how much locals had to share with tourists. Lisa created the "Greater Than a Tourist" book series to help connect people with locals. A topic that locals are very passionate about sharing.

Jeanne Croteau

> TOURIST

GREATER THAN A TOURIST

Notes

Made in the USA
Coppell, TX
12 October 2023